D0342782

THIS JOURNAL BELONGS TO

_____

I know that You can do all things,
and that no purpose of Yours can be thwarted.

Job 42:2 NASB

INTRODUCTION

Life throws us curveballs. Dreams get shaken by reality. We are sometimes put into situations we don't have the strength or wisdom to handle. But the good news is we don't have to! God loves it when we come to Him because we are at the end of ourselves. That's when we start relying on Him. He is God of the impossible. What He calls us to He will equip us for. He leans into us and encourages us to utilize His strength and His wisdom.

May the inspiring quotes and Scripture verses in this journal encourage you to trust God with the "impossibles" in your life!

When a problem looks insurmountable, God whispers, "Nothing is impossible for Me."

What is impossible with man is possible with God.

Luke 18:27 NIV

Keep your life so constant in its contact with God that His surprising power may break out on the right hand and on the left. Always be in a state of expectancy, and see that you leave room for God to come in as He likes.

Oswald Chambers

Trust in the Lord with all your heart, and lean not on your own understanding;
in all your ways acknowledge Him, and He shall direct your paths.

Proverbs 3:5–6 NKJV

While exploring God's goodness in the midst of a suffering world, I've taken the most pleasure in focusing on Him, exploring His attributes of goodness, love, holiness, justice, patience, grace, and mercy.

Randy Alcorn

Taste and see that the LORD is good; blessed is the one who takes refuge in him.
Fear the LORD, you his holy people, for those who fear him lack nothing.

Psalm 34:8–9 NIV

When you know what God says, what He means, and how to put His truths into practice, you will be equipped for every circumstance of life.

Kay Arthur

All Scripture is God-breathed and is useful for teaching, rebuking, correcting and training in righteousness, so that the servant of God may be thoroughly equipped for every good work.

2 Timothy 3:16–17 NIV

No storm is so great, no wave is so high, no sea is so deep, no wind is so strong, that Jesus cannot either calm it or carry us through it.

Anne Graham Lotz

Ah Lord God! Behold, You have made the heavens and the earth by
Your great power and by Your outstretched arm!
Nothing is too difficult for You.

Jeremiah 32:17 NASB

You and I can go to God when we are too tired, too lazy, too uncommitted, too sick, or feeling too sorry for ourselves. In fact, moments like these are precisely when we need to call upon God and be filled with His faithfulness.

Elizabeth George

Come to me, all who labor and are heavy laden, and I will give you rest. Take my yoke upon you, and learn from me, for I am gentle and lowly in heart, and you will find rest for your souls. For my yoke is easy, and my burden is light.

Matthew 11:28–30 ESV

If you believe in a God who controls the big things, you have to believe in a God who controls the little things. It is we, of course, to whom things look "little" or "big."
Elisabeth Elliot

Truly I tell you, if you have faith as small as a mustard seed, you can say to this mountain,
"Move from here to there," and it will move. Nothing will be impossible for you.

Matthew 17:20 NIV

When we are told that God, who is our dwelling place, is also our fortress, it can only mean one thing, and that is, that if we will but live in our dwelling place, we shall be perfectly safe and secure from every assault of every possible enemy that can attack us.
Hannah Whitall Smith

God is our refuge and strength, a very present help in trouble. Therefore we will not fear,
though the earth should change and though the mountains slip into the heart of the sea;
though its waters roar and foam, though the mountains quake at its swelling pride.

Psalm 46:1–3 NASB

Faith is the first factor in a life devoted to service. Without faith, nothing is possible. With it, nothing is impossible.

Mary McLeod Bethune

With God nothing will be impossible.

Luke 1:37 NKJV

Christian hope, unlike most other kinds of hope, is not mere optimism. It's not even a matter of thinking positively: "Cheer up. Things will work." Christian hope is applied faith. If God Himself is here with us in His Holy Spirit, then all things are possible.

Bruce Larson

May the God of hope fill you with all joy and peace as you trust in him,
so that you may overflow with hope by the power of the Holy Spirit.

Romans 15:13 NIV

Personal perfection is impossible, but it is possible to aim for genuineness, honesty, consistency, and moral purity, and to frankly acknowledge it when we fail.
Susan Alexander Yates

The Lord will perfect that which concerns me; Your mercy,
O Lord, endures forever; do not forsake the works of Your hands.

Psalm 138:8 NKJV

If our lives are easy, and if all we ever attempt for God is what we know we can handle, how will we ever experience His omnipotence in our lives?

Anne Graham Lotz

God has not given us a spirit of timidity, but of power and love and discipline.

2 Timothy 1:7 NASB

Nothing will ever be attempted if all possible objections must be first overcome.
Samuel Johnson

_____

_____

_____

_____

_____

_____

_____

_____

_____

_____

_____

_____

_____

_____

_____

_____

_____

_____

_____

_____

_____

_____

"My thoughts are nothing like your thoughts," says the Lord. "And my ways are far beyond anything you could imagine. For just as the heavens are higher than the earth, so my ways are higher than your ways and my thoughts higher than your thoughts."

Isaiah 55:8–9 NLT

A mother who walks with God knows He only asks her to take care of the possible and to trust Him with the impossible.

Ruth Bell Graham

Cast your cares on the LORD and he will sustain you;
he will never let the righteous be shaken.

Psalm 55:22 NIV

Jesus will give you a peace that you never imagined was possible...and a love that perfectly matches your constant wish.

Janet L. Smith

You will keep in perfect peace all who trust in you, all whose thoughts are fixed on you!

Isaiah 26:3 NLT

He only that stills the stormy seas can quiet the distressed and tempestuous soul.

John Flavel

Peace I leave with you; my peace I give you. I do not give to you as the world gives. Do not let your hearts be troubled and do not be afraid.

John 14:27 NIV

I was made for more than being stuck in a vicious cycle of defeat. I am not made to be a victim of my poor choices. I was made to be a victorious child of God.

Lysa TerKeurst

Thanks be to God, who gives us the victory through our Lord Jesus Christ.

1 Corinthians 15:57 ESV

Whatever it is,
However impossible it seems,
Whatever the obstacles that stand between you and it,
If it is noble,
If it is consistent with God's kingdom,
You must hunger after it
And stretch yourself to reach it.

Charles Paul Conn

It is God who arms me with strength and keeps my way secure.
He makes my feet like the feet of a deer; he causes me to stand on the heights.

Psalm 18:32–33 NIV

Since with God everything and anything are always possible,
be prepared to be surprised by wonders and miracles.

Everything is possible for one who believes.

Mark 9:23 NIV

If God wants you to do something, He'll make it possible for you to do it, but the grace He provides comes only with the task and cannot be stockpiled beforehand.
We are dependent on Him from hour to hour, and the greater our awareness of this fact, the less likely we are to faint or fail in a crisis.

Louis Cassels

Even the youths shall faint and be weary, and the young men shall utterly fall, but those who wait on the LORD shall renew their strength; they shall mount up with wings like eagles, they shall run and not be weary, they shall walk and not faint.

Isaiah 40:30–31 NKJV

Whenever Jesus calls on someone to get out of the boat,
He gives the power to walk on the water.

John Ortberg

The LORD himself goes before you and will be with you; he will never leave you nor forsake you. Do not be afraid; do not be discouraged.

Deuteronomy 31:8 NIV

When God is involved, anything can happen.... God has a beautiful way of bringing good vibrations out of broken chords.

Chuck Swindoll

The Spirit of the LORD God is upon Me...He has sent Me to heal the brokenhearted,
to proclaim liberty to the captives, and the opening of the prison to those who
are bound...to comfort all who mourn...to give them beauty for ashes,
the oil of joy for mourning, the garment of praise for the spirit of heaviness.

Isaiah 61:1–3 NKJV

God knows your value; He sees your potential. You may not understand everything you are going through right now. But hold your head up high, knowing that God is in control and He has a great plan and purpose for your life.

Joel Osteen

God had special plans for me and set me apart for his work.... He called me through his grace.

Galatians 1:15 NCV

To believe deeply...that God is present and at work in human life is to understand that I am a beloved child of this Father and, hence, free to trust. That makes a profound difference in the way I relate to myself and others; it makes an enormous different in the way I live.

Brennan Manning

We know that in all things God works for the good of those who love him,
who have been called according to his purpose.

Romans 8:28 NIV

Nothing is impossible for You. You hold my whole world in Your hands.
Kari Jobe

His divine power has given to us all things that pertain to life and godliness, through the knowledge of Him who called us by glory and virtue.

2 Peter 1:3 NKJV

Courage is fear that has said its prayers.

Dorothy Bernard

Do not fear, for I have redeemed you; I have summoned you by name; you are mine. When you pass through the waters, I will be with you; and when you pass through the rivers, they will not sweep over you. When you walk through the fire, you will not be burned; the flames will not set you ablaze. For I am the Lord your God, the Holy One of Israel, your Savior.

Isaiah 43:1-3 NIV

Success is determined not by whether or not you face obstacles, but by your reaction to them. And if you look at these obstacles as a containing fence, they become your excuse for failure. If you look at them as a hurdle, each one strengthens you for the next.

Ben Carson

*I, the LORD your God, hold your right hand; it is I who say to you,
"Fear not, I am the one who helps you."*

Isaiah 41:13 ESV

God will crush the obstacles in your life if you will follow in His way.

Jack Hayford

Thus says the Lord, your Redeemer, the Holy One of Israel,
"I am the Lord your God, who teaches you to profit,
Who leads you in the way you should go."

Isaiah 48:17–18 NASB

Let nothing disturb you, let nothing frighten you:
everything passes away except God; God alone is sufficient.
Teresa of Ávila

Don't panic. I'm with you. There's no need to fear for I'm your God. I'll give you strength.
I'll help you. I'll hold you steady, keep a firm grip on you.

Isaiah 41:10 MSG

Never be afraid to trust an unknown future to a known God.

Corrie ten Boom

Cast all your anxiety on him because he cares for you.

1 Peter 5:7 NIV

I am a God of abundance. I will never run out of resources;
My capacity to bless you is unlimited.

Sarah Young

Bless the Lord, O my soul, and forget not all His benefits: who forgives all your iniquities, who heals all your diseases, who redeems your life from destruction, who crowns you with lovingkindness and tender mercies, who satisfies your mouth with good things, so that your youth is renewed like the eagle's.

Psalm 103:2–5 NKJV

You have been created by God and for God, and someday you will stand amazed at the simple yet profound ways He has used you even when you weren't aware of it.

Kay Arthur

God loves you, and we know he has chosen you.

1 Thessalonians 1:4 NCV

Our days are in God's hands. He is all-sufficient to meet our needs,
and the Savior is with us every step of the way.

Elizabeth George

The Lord directs the steps of the godly. He delights in every detail of their lives.

Psalm 37:23 NLT

Deny your weakness, and you will never realize God's strength in you.

Joni Eareckson Tada

He said to me, "My grace is sufficient for you, for my power is made perfect in weakness."
Therefore I will boast all the more gladly about my weaknesses,
so that Christ's power may rest on me.... For when I am weak, then I am strong.

2 Corinthians 12:9–10 NIV

In Jesus the weak are strong, and the defenseless safe; they could not be more strong if they were giants, or more safe if they were in heaven. Faith gives to men on earth the protection of the God of heaven.

Charles H. Spurgeon

Everyone who has been born of God overcomes the world.
And this is the victory that has overcome the world—our faith.

1 John 5:4 ESV

When faced with a mountain, I will not quit! I will keep on striving until I climb over, find a pass through, tunnel underneath, or simply stay and turn the mountain into a gold mine with God's help.

Dr. Robert Schuller

You will light my lamp; the LORD my God will enlighten my darkness.
For by You I can run against a troop, by my God I can leap over a wall.

Psalm 18:28–29 NKJV

If we want to see mighty wonders of divine power and grace wrought in the place of weakness, failure, and disappointment, let us answer God's standing challenge, "Call unto me, and I will answer you, and show you great and mighty things that you know not!"

J. Hudson Taylor

_____

_____

_____

_____

_____

_____

_____

_____

_____

_____

_____

_____

_____

_____

_____

_____

_____

_____

_____

_____

_____

_____

_____

The LORD says, "I will rescue those who love me. I will protect those who trust in my name.
When they call on me, I will answer; I will be with them in trouble. I will rescue and honor them.
I will reward them with a long life and give them my salvation."

Psalm 91:14-16 NLT

With God our trust can be abandoned, utterly free. In Him are no limitations, no flaws, no weaknesses. His judgment is perfect, His knowledge of us is perfect, His love is perfect. God alone is trustworthy.

Eugenia Price

Those who know your name trust in you,
for you, LORD, have never forsaken those who seek you.

Psalm 9:10 NIV

I feel simply carried along each hour, doing my part in a plan which is far beyond myself. This sense of cooperation with God in little things is what so astonishes me, for I never have felt this way before. I need something, and turn around to find it waiting for me. I must work, to be sure, but there is God working along with me.

Frank Laubach

Trust in the LORD, and do good; dwell in the land, and feed on His faithfulness....
Commit your way to the LORD, trust also in Him, and He shall bring it to pass.
He shall bring forth your righteousness as the light, and your justice as the noonday.

Psalm 37:3, 5–6 NKJV

You ought to act with God in the greatest simplicity. Speak to Him frankly and plainly. Implore His assistance in your affairs just as they are happening: He will never fail to grant it.

Brother Lawrence

Call upon Me in the day of trouble; I shall rescue you, and you will honor Me.

A "prayer warrior" is a person who is convinced that God is omnipotent—that God has the power to do anything, to change anyone, and to intervene in any circumstance. A person who truly believes this refuses to doubt God.

Bill Hybels

Is anything too hard for the LORD?

Genesis 18:14 NIV

It is not what we do that matters, but what a sovereign God chooses to do through us. God doesn't want our success; He wants us.

Charles Colson

Unless the Lord builds the house, the builders labor in vain.
Unless the Lord watches over the city, the guards stand watch in vain.

Psalm 127:1 NIV

The "air" which our souls need also envelops all of us at all times and on all sides.
God is round about us in Christ on every hand, with many-sided and all-sufficient
grace. All we need to do is to open our hearts.

Ole Hallesby

*God is able to make all grace abound toward you, that you, always having
all sufficiency in all things, may have an abundance for every good work.*

2 Corinthians 9:8 NKJV

Without God, we cannot. Without us, God will not.

Augustine

I can do all things through Him who strengthens me.

Philippians 4:13 NASB

We don't have to be perfect.... We are asked only to be real, trusting in His perfection to cover our imperfection, knowing that one day we will finally be all that Christ saved us for and wants us to be.

Gigi Graham Tchividjian

Those who seek the LORD lack no good thing.

Psalm 34:10 NIV

We sometimes fear to bring our troubles to God, because they must seem so small to Him who sits on the circle of the earth. But if they are large enough to...endanger our welfare, they are large enough to touch His heart of love.

R. A. Torrey

The Lord is near to all who call upon Him, to all who call upon Him in truth.
He will fulfill the desire of those who fear Him; He also will hear their cry and save them.

Psalm 145:18–19 NKJV

It is not my ability, but my response to God's ability, that counts.

Corrie ten Boom

*Do you not know? Have you not heard? The L*ORD *is the everlasting God, the Creator of the ends of the earth. He will not grow tired or weary, and his understanding no one can fathom. He gives strength to the weary and increases the power of the weak.*

Isaiah 40:28-29 NIV

In difficulties, I can drink freely of God's power and experience His touch of
refreshment and blessing—much like an invigorating early spring rain.
Anabel Gillham

Surely God is my salvation; I will trust and not be afraid. The LORD, the LORD himself,
is my strength and my defense; he has become my salvation.
With joy you will draw water from the wells of salvation.

Isaiah 12:2–3 NIV

No matter how many times you get knocked down, keep getting back up. God sees your resolve. He sees your determination. And when you do everything you can do, that's when God will step in and do what you can't do.

Joel Osteen

Let us not lose heart in doing good, for in due time we will reap if we do not grow weary.

Galatians 6:9 NASB

God is looking for people who will come in simple dependence upon His grace, and rest in simple faith upon His greatness. At this very moment, He's looking at you.
Jack Hayford

_____

_____

_____

_____

_____

_____

_____

_____

_____

_____

_____

_____

_____

_____

_____

The eyes of the LORD range throughout the earth to strengthen those whose hearts are fully committed to him.

2 Chronicles 16:9 NIV

Grasp the fact that God is for you—let this certainty make its impact on you in relation to what you are up against at this very moment; and you will find in thus knowing God as your sovereign protector, irrevocably committed to you in the covenant of grace, both freedom from fear and new strength for the fight.

J. I. Packer

Now may our Lord Jesus Christ Himself and God our Father, who has loved us and given us eternal comfort and good hope by grace, comfort and strengthen your hearts in every good work and word.

2 Thessalonians 2:16–17 NASB

When you are tempted to give up, your breakthrough is probably just around the corner.

Joyce Meyer

Be strong and take heart, all you who hope in the LORD.

Psalm 31:24 NIV

God is a rich and bountiful Father, and He does not forget His children, nor withhold from them anything which it would be to their advantage to receive.

J. K. Maclean

My God will meet all your needs according to the riches of his glory in Christ Jesus.

Philippians 4:19 NIV

Where human help is at an end, God's help begins.
Martin Luther

As for me, I will always have hope; I will praise you more and more.

Strength, rest, guidance, grace, help, sympathy, love—all from God to us!
What a list of blessings!

Evelyn Stenbock

You will show me the path of life; in your presence is fullness of joy; at your right hand are pleasures forevermore.

Psalm 16:11 NKJV

Lift up your eyes. Your heavenly Father waits to bless you—in inconceivable ways to make your life what you never dreamed it could be.

Anne Ortlund

No eye has seen, no ear has heard, and no mind has imagined
what God has prepared for those who love him.

1 Corinthians 2:9 NLT

God is waiting for us to come to Him with our needs.... God's throne room is always open.... Every single believer in the whole world could walk into the throne room all at one time, and it would not even be crowded.

Charles Stanley

Be anxious for nothing, but in everything by prayer and supplication, with thanksgiving, let your requests be made known to God; and the peace of God, which surpasses all understanding, will guard your hearts and minds through Christ Jesus.

Philippians 4:6–7 NKJV

Regardless of whether we feel strong or weak in our faith, we remember that our assurance is not based upon our ability to conjure up some special feeling. Rather, it is built upon a confident assurance in the faithfulness of God. We focus on His trustworthiness and especially on His steadfast love.

Richard J. Foster

Because of the Lord's great love we are not consumed, for his compassions never fail.
They are new every morning; great is your faithfulness.

Lamentations 3:22-23 NIV

So faith bounds forward to its goal in God, and love can trust her Lord to lead her there;
upheld by Him my soul is following hard, till God has fully fulfilled my deepest prayer.

Frederick Brook

My soul follows close behind You; Your right hand upholds me.

Psalm 63:8 NKJV

Trust in your Redeemer's strength...exercise what faith you have, and by and by He shall rise upon you with healing beneath His wings. Go from faith to faith and you shall receive blessing upon blessing.

Charles H. Spurgeon

The Lord is my strength and my shield; my heart trusts in him, and he helps me.
My heart leaps for joy, and with my song I praise him.

Psalm 28:7 NIV

There is this fine line between presenting to You all of my weakness and thinking that it can't be done. In Your strength, I find my own.

Joni Eareckson Tada

The Sovereign LORD is my strength; he makes my feet like the feet of a deer,
he enables me to tread on the heights.

Habakkuk 3:19 NIV

Successful people don't have fewer problems. They have determined that nothing will stop them from going forward.

Ben Carson

He who calls you is faithful, who also will do it.

1 Thessalonians 5:24 NKJV

The most glorious promises of God are generally fulfilled in such a wondrous manner that He steps forth to save us at a time when there is the least appearance of it.

Karl Heinrich von Bogatzky

Behold, I am doing a new thing; now it springs forth, do you not perceive it?
I will make a way in the wilderness and rivers in the desert.

Isaiah 43:19 ESV

God is the God of promise. He keeps His word, even when that seems impossible.
Colin Urquhart

The LORD is trustworthy in all he promises and faithful in all he does.
The LORD upholds all who fall and lifts up all who are bowed down.

Psalm 145:13-14 NIV

We know that if we call on the Lord He will answer. Often, however, our expectations are too small, and we ask based on what we know is possible. But He is the God of the impossible! The Lord sees the situation from every side and has a bigger plan than any of us dream. He did not choose us to do small things.

Jack Hayford

Call to Me and I will answer you, and I will tell you great and mighty things, which you do not know.

Jeremiah 33:3 NASB

God has plans for you and His plans are for good because God Himself is good.

Elizabeth George

"For I know the plans I have for you," declares the LORD, "plans to prosper you and not to harm you, plans to give you hope and a future."

Jeremiah 29:11 NIV

We walk without fear, full of hope and courage and strength to do His will, waiting for the endless good which He is always giving as fast as He can get us able to take it in.
George MacDonald

The Lord longs to be gracious to you; therefore he will rise up to show you compassion.
For the Lord is a God of justice. Blessed are all who wait for him!

Isaiah 30:18 NIV

Outside our comfort zone...is where we experience the true awesomeness of God.
Lysa TerKeurst

*I have set the L*ORD *continually before me; because He is at my right hand, I will not be shaken.*

Psalm 16:8 NASB

When we are powerless to do a thing, it is a great joy that we can come and step inside the ability of Jesus.

Corrie ten Boom

My flesh and my heart fail; but God is the strength of my heart and my portion forever.

Psalm 73:26 NKJV

To live your best life now, you must learn to trust God's timing. You may not think He's working, but you can be sure that right now, behind the scenes, God is arranging all the pieces to come together to work out His plan for your life.

Joel Osteen

_Being confident of this, that he who began a good work in you
will carry it on to completion until the day of Christ Jesus._

Philippians 1:6 NIV

The cross did what man could not do. It granted us the right to talk with, love, and even live with God.

Max Lucado

I trust in your unfailing love; my heart rejoices in your salvation.

Psalm 13:5 NIV

When we focus on God, the scene changes. He's in control of our lives; nothing lies outside the realm of His redemptive grace. Even when we make mistakes, fail in relationships, or deliberately make bad choices, God can redeem us.

Penelope J. Stokes

Seek first His kingdom and His righteousness, and all these things will be added to you.

Matthew 6:33 NASB

Our feelings do not affect God's facts. They may blow up, like clouds, and cover the eternal things that we do most truly believe. We may not see the shining of the promises—but they still shine! [His strength] is not for one moment less because of our human weakness.

Amy Carmichael

The LORD is my strength and my shield;
in him my heart trusts, and I am helped;
my heart exults, and with my song I give thanks to him.

Psalm 28:7 ESV

We know that [God] gives us every grace, every abundant grace; and though we are so weak of ourselves, this grace is able to carry us through every obstacle and difficulty.

Elizabeth Ann Seton

Let us then approach God's throne of grace with confidence, so that we may receive mercy and find grace to help us in our time of need.

Hebrews 4:16 NIV

Each of us may be sure that if God sends us on stony paths He will provide us with strong shoes, and He will not send us out on any journey for which He does not equip us well.
Alexander Maclaren

The Lord God is a sun and shield; the Lord will give grace and glory; no good thing will He withhold from those who walk uprightly.

Psalm 84:11 NKJV

We have a Father in heaven who is almighty, who loves His children...and whose very joy and delight it is to...help them at all times.

George Mueller

This is your Father you are dealing with, and he knows better than you what you need.
With a God like this loving you, you can pray very simply.

Matthew 6:7 MSG

If you are a child of God whose heart's desire is to see God glorified through you, adversity will not put you down for the count. There will be those initial moments of shock and confusion. But the man or woman who has God's perspective on this life and the life to come will always emerge victorious!

Charles Stanley

Our light affliction, which is but for a moment, is working for us a far more exceeding and eternal weight of glory, while we do not look at the things which are seen, but at the things which are not seen. For the things which are seen are temporary, but the things which are not seen are eternal.

2 Corinthians 4:17–18 NKJV

Our God specializes in working through normal people who believe in a supernormal God who will do His work through them.

Bruce Wilkinson

You have worked wonders, plans formed long ago, with perfect faithfulness.

Isaiah 25:1 NASB

Ellie Claire™ Gift & Paper Expressions
Brentwood, TN 37027
EllieClaire.com

With God All Things Are Possible Journal
© 2014 by Ellie Claire, an imprint of Worthy Media, Inc.

ISBN 978-1-60936-935-4

All rights reserved. No part of this book may be reproduced in any form, except for brief quotations in printed reviews, without permission in writing from the publisher.

The Holy Bible, New International Version®, NIV®. Copyright © 1973, 1978, 1984, 2011 by Biblica, Inc.® All rights reserved worldwide. The Holy Bible, New King James Version® (NKJV). Copyright © 1982 by Thomas Nelson, Inc. The Holy Bible, English Standard Version® (ESV®), copyright © 2001 by Crossway Bibles, a publishing ministry of Good News Publishers. The New American Standard Bible® (NASB), copyright © 1960, 1962, 1963, 1968, 1971, 1972, 1973, 1975, 1977, 1995 by The Lockman Foundation. The Holy Bible, New Living Translation (NLT), copyright 1996, 2004, 2007 by Tyndale House Foundation. Used by permission of Tyndale House Publishers, Inc., Carol Stream, Illinois 60188. *The Message* (MSG). Copyright © 1993, 1994, 1995, 1996, 2000, 2001, 2002. Used by permission of NavPress Publishing Group. The New Century Version® (NCV). Copyright © 2005 by Thomas Nelson, Inc. Used by permission. All rights reserved.

Excluding Scripture verses and deity pronouns, in some quotations references to men and masculine pronouns have been replaced with gender-neutral or feminine references. Additionally, in some quotations we have carefully updated verb forms and wording that may distract modern readers.

Stock or custom editions of Ellie Claire titles may be purchased in bulk for educational, business, ministry, fundraising, or sales promotional use. For information, please e-mail info@EllieClaire.com.

Cover image: Thinkstock Images

Compiled by Jill Jones.
Cover and interior design by Gearbox | StudioGearbox.com.

Printed in China.

1 2 3 4 5 6 7 8 9 – 19 18 17 16 15 14